Y0-CKH-302

MAR 19	DATE DUE		

629.22

TALYOR, RICH

CAFE RACERS

**WATERLOO LOCAL SCHOOL
MIDDLE SCHOOL LIBRARY**

A GOLDEN WHEELS BOOK
Café Racers
Customs/Production Bikes/Road Racers

Rich Taylor
Photography by TAYLOR-CONSTANTINE

GOLDEN PRESS/NEW YORK
Western Publishing Company, Inc., Racine, Wisconsin

Library of Congress Catalog Card Number: 75-37103

Copyright © 1976 by Western Publishing Company, Inc.
All rights reserved. No part of this book may be reproduced or copied in any form without written permission from the publisher.
Printed in U.S.A.

Golden, a Golden Book® and Golden Press® are trademarks of Western Publishing Company, Inc.

Foreword

A café racer is, in the simplest definition, a street legal motorcycle that captures some of the aura of a genuine road racer. But like most simple definitions, this one hardly covers every facet. Factory technicians with unlimited funds might produce a machine loosely based on the motorcycles they sell for everyday transportation—a handbuilt 170 mph AMA Championship racer with a headlight. And they can call it a café racer. But the kid down the block can add a few fiberglass bits to his old street wobbler . . . and he'll have a café racer, too. In between, there are dozens of true dual-purpose machines that people ride to work during the week, and perhaps run in "production" races over the weekend . . . or in informal Sunday morning contests with friends on any empty, back-country road. The variations are virtually endless. Because "café racer" is such an indefinite term, any bike that someone *thinks* looks like a road racer *to him* is a legitimate café racer. And since most are custom built, there's no such thing as a standard format. It's strictly Road Racer Free Form at every level.

The heart of any motorcycle is the engine. And because a café racer is a special cycle, the engine should be special, too. Ducatis with exotic desmodromic valve gear qualify right out of the crate, while something like the Laverda Three is so technologically superior, so overwhelming as it comes from the factory, there's little to improve. For more common powerplants like the various Honda Fours and the Kawasaki Z-1, there are legions of after-market machinists turning out trick speed parts to build engines that range from barely warm, cooking versions to full-race blast furnaces with an overabundance of sheer, brute horsepower. At the small end of the scale, Yamaha makes 250cc and 350cc Twins for the street that are just a slim remove from the race track. Do a little work on the carbs and ports, and you can ride a miniracer that's nearly the equal of AMA Championship Yamahas—and more than a match for most larger machines you'd encounter on the street.

With the almost universal adoption of disc brakes by bike manufacturers, it's not hard to find good braking for a café racer—double-disc conversion kits, cool-running radially drilled discs, coated aluminum discs . . . almost any refinement your pocketbook will stand. The same goes for the chassis. It gets expensive to build a whole new frame for a café racer, and the technology is beyond the means of most backyard mechanics. But specialist firms like Seeley, Rickman, Dresda and Egli make exquisite—albeit expensive—

photo courtesy of Doug Mesney

frames that work better than what comes wrapped around the average motorcycle. Not that modern frames are all that bad. Yamaha uses the same geometry in its street frames as its road racers. And most other street machines can be easily improved. Better tires and shock absorbers, balanced spring rates, carefully selected fork oil viscosity... a multitude of little suspension changes can make a bike go around corners more quickly.

Rider position has a lot to do with café racer performance and appearance. A racing seat that positively locates you at high speeds, rear-set footpegs and clip-on bars will radically change the weight distribution. Frame-mounted fairings are convenient, look supremely racy and barely affect performance in the speed ranges café racers can hit on the street.

Depending on the inherent weaknesses of whatever bike you start building your café racer from, different parts will need modifying and replacing. But this is usually an on-going process. It's a rare café racer whose owner considers it finished. There will always be a new tach bracket, a better set of footpegs or a fancier paint job to tempt the owner into tearing it all apart once more. Even the factory café racers—and there are half a dozen or more now available—inevitably receive a few finishing touches at the hands of their proud new owners.

For the essence of the café racer is the image the *rider* wants to project, not the image the factory wants to project for him. So while a factory café racer is usually a better machine than a backyard tuner could build, it's not necessarily a better machine for that particular rider. If it doesn't do something special for *him*, alone, he might as well be tooling around on a stock Honda. In the final analysis, it's that tangible feeling of confidence you get from a well-crafted machine that's most important. And that comes from a motorcycle that's distinctive, capable and well thought out. If your café racer inspires trust and affection, it's probably the right one.

Now none of the specific machines in this gallery of representative café racers is going to be *The One*. The idea is to chronicle what's being done, what some of today's best ideas are and what it's possible to do with the funds available. The most expensive bike in this book costs somewhere over $27,000 to build... the cheapest could be duplicated for under $1,000. Despite their obvious differences, both are street legal bikes (just barely in some respects) that capture the elusive essence of what constitutes a road-racing motorcycle. And that alone makes them café racers.

Ducati 350 Desmo GT

Sometimes it seems like *every* Italian rider thinks he's Giacomo Agostini, and every road the parabolic at Monza. The end result of this happy madness is a whole flotilla of high performance street bikes, all deserving to be called café racers. In Italy they range from watercooled 50cc wonders to 1000cc monsters.

In the middle range, perhaps the best of all Italian café racers is the single-cylinder Ducati 350, with desmodromic valve gear. This particular silver machine is a limited-production factory design that is trickier than many customs. It features exquisitely fabricated rear-sets and controls, clip-on Tomaselli bars and a huge fiberglass tank with matching seat and front fender. The seat conceals a handy storage box, but virtually every other part is right out in the open. Although tiny, this Ducati's mechanical presence is that of a much greater machine. Not as impressive as a Ducati 750 Super Sport, it still has an eminence all its own.

It was originally imported by Steve Wilkinson, the New York-based editor of *Car and Driver* magazine, later passed to Burge Hulett in Florida and now resides in Cedar Rapids, Iowa, with Ducati collector Bob Westerkamp. Bob also has a matching metal-flake full fairing and open megaphone exhaust which can be easily bolted on to push the lightweight Ducati well over 100 mph. And because of the bike's inherent simplicity, it's also been surprisingly reliable and easy to service.

The basic Ducati design has been around for ages, and the little Single, even with positive closing desmodromic valves, doesn't really create very much power. But the handling more than makes up for this deficiency. Available only on special order in this country, the Ducati GT is a more-than-competent miniracer with loads of traditional character . . . and of course, that special sound only a four-stroke Single can produce.

Ducati 350 Desmo Mark III

Very similar to Westerkamp's machine, this Mark III Desmo 350 was put together by Los Angeles machinist Bob Norton. Starting with a stock Ducati street machine, Norton has added a leather-covered fiberglass dual seat, making this one of the few small café racers around that accommodates a passenger. The flat handlebars aren't as racy as clip-ons, but they're a lot more comfortable . . . particularly with stock position footpegs. A Filtron air filter sticking out the right side is about the only other conspicuous change visible to those who aren't ardent Ducati mavens. Those who know "Ducks," though, will notice an incredible amount of careful detailing in the paint, chrome and control cables—almost imperceptible improvements that enhance the bike's inherent good looks.

Yamaha 350 R-5

Dunstall is a name that's usually associated with speed parts for big Nortons and Triumphs, but this little Yamaha 350 built by Max Gordon's International Cycles in San Jose has more than the usual dose of Dunstall equipment. The angular fiberglass dual seat/oversized tank combination is straight Dunstall, as is the matching front fender. The stock rear fender has been cut to fit the Dunstall seat, which hides a surprisingly large storage bin tucked beneath a squarish trap door behind the padding. Rear-sets have been built around the stock passenger footpegs and pivot on aircraft-quality Heim joints. New folding passenger pegs attach to the lower shock mounts for occasional use. Dunstall clubman handlebars that approximate the feel of clip-ons—though using the stock mounts—are used at the front, along with new chrome headlight brackets and a flat-black headlamp shell that matches the similar sidecovers and dramatic styling of the stock Yamaha engine.

The only performance changes are free-flow aircleaners and J&R muffled chrome expansion chambers, but they're more than enough to take the chill off Yamaha's already potent, piston-port Twin. Although lacking the reed valves and front disc brake of the current RD-350, this Dunstallized Yamaha seems more than satisfactory as a slick street racer.

Yamaha RD-350

Used as a showcase for the Fibercraft seat, tank, fairing and fender manufactured by Dick Kilgroe, this pristine white RD-350 belongs to Rube Goldberg Distributing, a Los Angeles café racer emporium. The 4.5 gallon tank is a production version of a racing tank first built for Suzuki's 250cc road racers, while the seat is the same as those built by Fibercraft for Kawasaki factory road racers. The fairing's trickiest feature is a streamlined, clear plexiglass nose cone that covers the headlight and adds a couple of miles per hour to the bike's top speed. The rear-sets are by Starbiker; the clubman bar is the expensive Dunstall.

The chassis of this Yamaha is toughly built box stock; and it gets flogged daily as a dealer demonstration model. With six speeds, reed valve carburetors and disc brake, though, Yamaha's 350 is a lot more motorcycle than many bikes twice its size, just as it comes from the factory. And for those who want to go *really* fast, the mail-order performance available for these Yamahas is limited only by the extent of your imagination . . . and your bank account.

Yamaha RD-350

Unlike many café racers, this RD-350 Yamaha has been put together with an emphasis on function. The appearance pretty much just happened. This is only logical, though, since it was built primarily as a "production" road racer rather than a street bike. Crafted by Long Island tuner "Fast John" Baugh for THEM Racing, it has run over 125 mph at Daytona International. It's been warmed over with a balanced crankshaft, road-race porting, K&K aircleaners and completely micro-sealed engine. The wet clutch has heavy-duty springs and will safely handle 10,000 rpm, an obtainable speed even with the Yamaha's restrictive street silencers. The rear shocks are Koni, with Tim Witham springs.

At the front, reworked damping is concealed beneath reversed fork legs which put the disc brake caliper behind the fork leg for better handling. And the disc itself has been radially drilled for increased cooling. Dunlop road-racing tires are fitted, along with a 39-tooth rear sprocket. Only a tachometer is used, fitted to a custom bracket angled to the rear for better visibility. The bars are Dunstall Clubmans, legal for "production" class racing since they utilize the stock mounting points. Practical rear-sets have been built around the stock passenger footpegs, while the old-fashioned seat is a Bates product, covered in blue leather to match the racing suits of the team's riders. Understandably, this deceptively modest RD-350 is a real sleeper on the street.

Seeley-Matchless 500

If the THEM Yamaha represents the victory of artless two-stroke technology over the aesthetic craftsmanship of the old-timers, this Seeley-Matchless must surely personify the opposite extreme. Built by master cycle builder Frank Reps of Los Angeles, it's easily one of the most beautiful of traditional café racers. The lightweight, plated racing frame (with no downtubes), the slim fiberglass tank and unusually angular dual seat were all developed by British specialty manufacturer Colin Seeley. Six of these frame kits were produced in 1971, designed to accept the beloved old G-50 Matchless 500cc four-stroke Single that—along with the similar Manx Norton Single—formed the backbone of English and American privateer road racing long before the Italians and Japanese raised the stakes to today's high levels.

Reps' Matchless has a time-honored Amal GP carb on an extra-long intake stack and a custom exhaust ending in a stock Norton Commando street muffler. The separate gearbox is a Quaife close-ratio, 5-speed conversion for the archaic AMC 4-speed as used by Norton, Matchless and AJS. With road-race gearing, first gear is good for over 40 mph, and top speed is about 125 mph. Avon Speedmaster tires, AMC forks and Girling shocks are the traditional English formula for high speed road work, and they perform brilliantly. Best of all, Reps' old Seeley—complete with Manx Norton fender, Smiths tach and Matchless ventilated front drum brake—is an absolute ball to ride. A purebred British Single is far and away more fun to ride than most bikes . . . and Rep's Seeley is without doubt the ultimate "thumper."

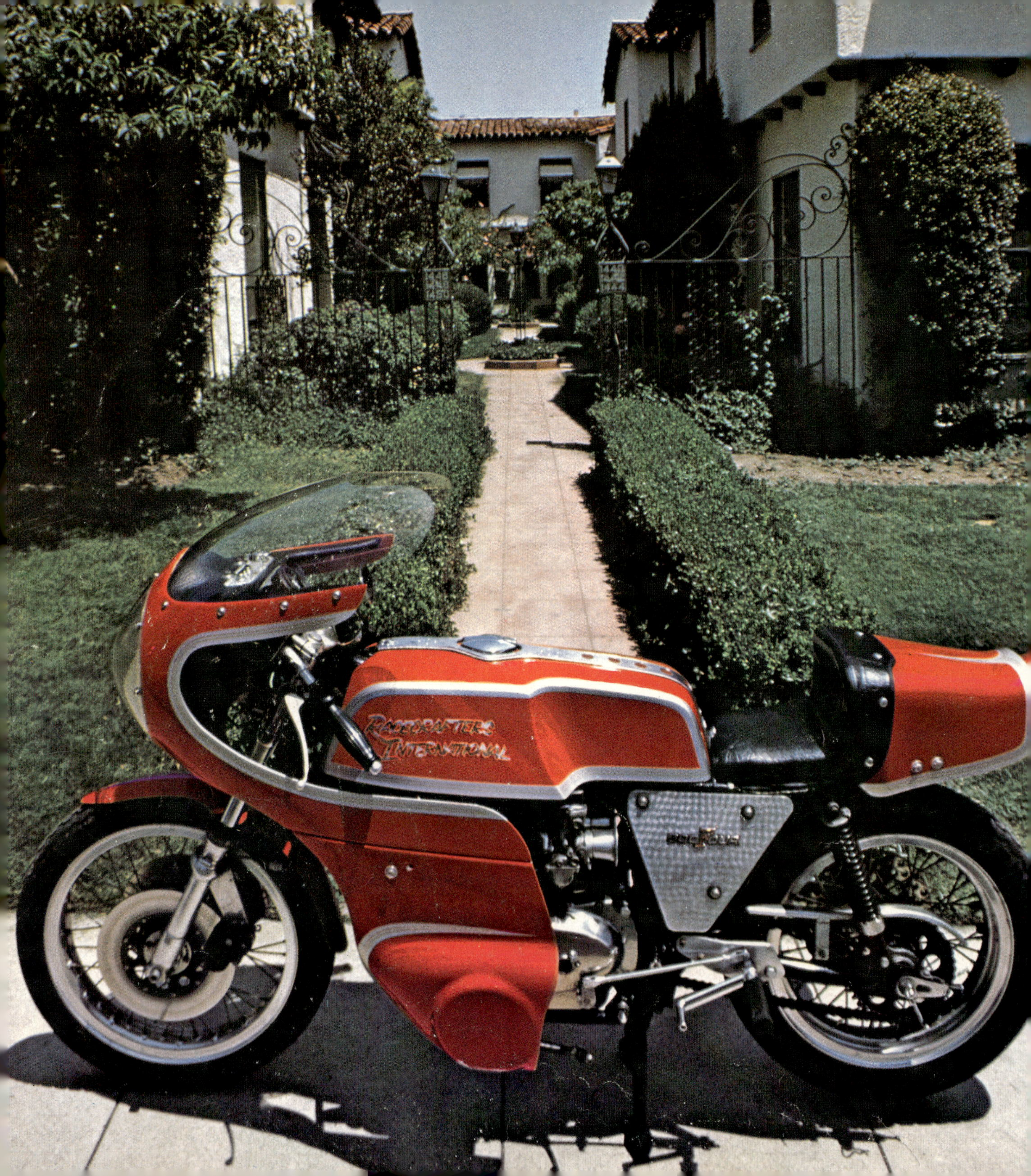
RACECRAFTERS
INTERNATIONAL

Honda CB-550

Built by Bob Faniff for Lyn Abrams—the owner of Racecrafters International on Hollywood's Sunset Strip—this incredible Honda 550 is one of the most perfect assemblages of motorcycle parts in the world. Almost every component is the finest money can buy. The frame is a stock 1973 Honda, fitted with Ceriani front forks, dual Honda front discs, Borrani alloy rims and road-racing Dunlop tires. The headlight is a Marchal quartz-iodine unit, fitted into a Read-Titan full fairing. The clip-ons are Tomaselli, the instruments a custom-built conglomeration of Honda and Stewart-Warner. The huge 5.0-gallon tank is also from Read-Titan, crafted from stainless steel rather than fiberglass. The seat is a Fibercraft product sold by Racecrafters, while the sidecovers are engine-turned aluminum built by Faniff. The rear-sets are John Tickle units made in England. The rear Borrani rim laces to a Barnes hub with quick-change sprocket and is fitted with a Dunlop K-81 and a ventilated Hurst-Airheart disc. Koni shocks and Witham springs complete the rear. The engine of this mind-boggling composite is a Yoshimura-built Honda Four, fitted with every conceivable performance option, from velocity stacks and Isle-of-Man cam to Kerker four-into-one megaphone exhaust. Whether the five-figure pricetag is worth it, only you can decide.

Honda CB-550

This bright extravaganza is a carefully smoothed Honda 550, with one of the softest pearlescent paint jobs you can imagine. It virtually glows in the dark. The two-passenger seat is an expanded version of Fibercraft's fancy Kawasaki racing seat; and the fat, pumpkin tank is from the same place. The fairing is one of Paul Dunstall's new and rather awkward bits of molding that's currently coming into vogue, with a distinctive, sharply-cornered trapezoidal hole for the headlight. For the rest, this Rube Goldberg Distributing Honda is conventional California Café, from Dunlop K-81s to Kerker four-into-one exhaust, Fibercrafter front fender to Starbiker rear-sets.

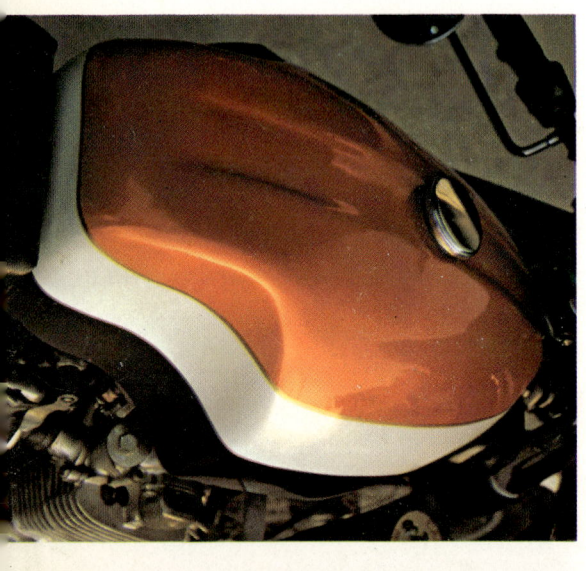

Ducati 750 Sport

Among all the factory-built, big-bore café racers, two of the best have Ducati nameplates. The less exotic of the pair is the 750 Sport, and it's a more serious piece of machinery than many supposedly more exotic cycles. The V-twin engine is used as a structural member as on all Ducatis, big and small, with the downtubes bolted to the front of the crankcase. It's not the most attractive powerplant in the world, but it does have surprising reserves of torque and horsepower. It does lack the electric starter that most other big bikes now consider standard equipment, and it also lacks air cleaners—a real shame on a machine with hand-worked internals.

The front forks are built by Ceriani, the rims are Borrani, the clip-ons by Tomaselli. An excellent front disc brake mounts to Ducati's own beautifully cast alloy hub. Similar craftsmanship is in evidence throughout, from the lightweight fender to the superbly styled fiberglass rear seat that blends perfectly with the equally stunning bulbous Italian tank. With great handling, lots of power and an efficient—if cramped—riding position tendered by hand-knurled rearsets and carefully worked controls, the Ducati Sport is so good as it comes from the factory that there's not much left to fiddle with.

Ducati 750 Super Sport

The 750 Super Sport is Ducati's own idea of how to make a *real* café racer out of its already impressive Ducati Sport. The Super Sport is generally acknowledged as just about the finest two-wheeled experience you can buy for upwards of $5,000 . . . if you can locate one of these rare machines for sale. Most seem to go to "friends of the factory."

Like the smaller Ducati 350 Desmo GT (the 750 V-twin is really two 350 Singles on a common crankcase), the Super Sport is fitted with elaborate overhead cam-operated desmodromic valves. Most of the chassis is identical to that on the cheaper 750 Sport, though a second disc brake has been added on the front wheel and a hydraulically operated single disc replaces the Sport's rear drum. The huge gas tank is a marvelously styled container, in the functionally fat tradition of Italian road-racing machinery.

A neat little trick is the clear plastic strip molded into the side— a built-in gas gauge. The lovely little bikini fairing is standard on the Super Sport, painted in subtle silver and teal blue. All in all, you'd have to know as much about high speed motorcycles as the combined Ducati factory racing department to come up yourself with a café racer that's as good.

Rickman-Royal Enfield 750

Don and Derek Rickman have long been famous for their exquisite nickel-plated Metisse frame kits. Available for a variety of popular powerplants, these component kits need only engine, chain, mufflers, instruments and electrics to complete. The lovely full fairing, the long, slender gas tank, the seat and front fender are all Rickman's own fiberglass. Even the front and rear Lockheed disc brakes, Girling shocks, Dunlop tires, alloy rims and custom front forks are included in the admittedly steep price of the Rickman package.

Most of them end up propelled by Triumph Twins, but Dick LaPlante has a more exotic version, built around a similar Royal Enfield 750 Twin. Since Dick's Cycle West in San Gabriel owns a fair portion of the world's supply of orphaned Enfield engines and Rickman/Enfield frames, it's only logical that this showpiece should have originated there. The warmed-over Enfield has lots of long-stroke torque and makes a lovely sound.

More graceful than Rickman's latest Honda and Kawasaki kits, the original Metisse is a real aesthetic tour de force . . . not to mention one of the best handling chassis ever designed. Rare, exotic and expensive, these early Rickman frames are still in small-batch production . . . and understandably high demand.

Honda CB-750

If the natural habitat for a thoroughly British Rickman/Enfield Metisse is in front of a pub in Douglas, on the Isle of Man, then Ed Safire's Honda 750 Four belongs squarely in front of Grauman's Chinese Theatre on Sunset Strip. It's a genuine "Kalifornia Kustom Kafé Racer" stretched to its glittering, costly zenith. Safire's Honda has absorbed two full years of work and somewhere over $7,000, and yet—unbelievably—it's served as street transportation for the entire period of construction.

Most striking is the one-piece Tracy Fiberglass seat and tank combination, covered in two dozen coats of Candyapple metalflake, shadow-fogged, pinstriped lacquer. But the paint is just the beginning. The stock Honda Four has been polished, painted and plated until there's very little left of what originally left Japan. As an example of Safire's attention to detail, notice that all the carburetor bodies and adjustment screws have been *chromed* . . . not to mention obvious things like aircraft quality fuel lines, plated allen-head sidecover bolts, etc. The cast magnesium "snowflake" wheels are from TimKab, fitted with Dunlop TT100 tires. The rear disc is also a TimKab, but if you look closely you'll notice the double front discs are chrome. Safire obtained aircraft hard chrome and machined it to fit the cast wheel. The exhaust is a chromed Kerker, the controls are Tomaselli and the triple clamp, headlamp brackets and rear-sets are all custom built. And that adds up to thousands of man hours invested in swiss-cheesed brake caliper brackets, a custom cover for the unused kickstarter shaft, and so on. But then, what's time or money to an artist obsessed by his creation?

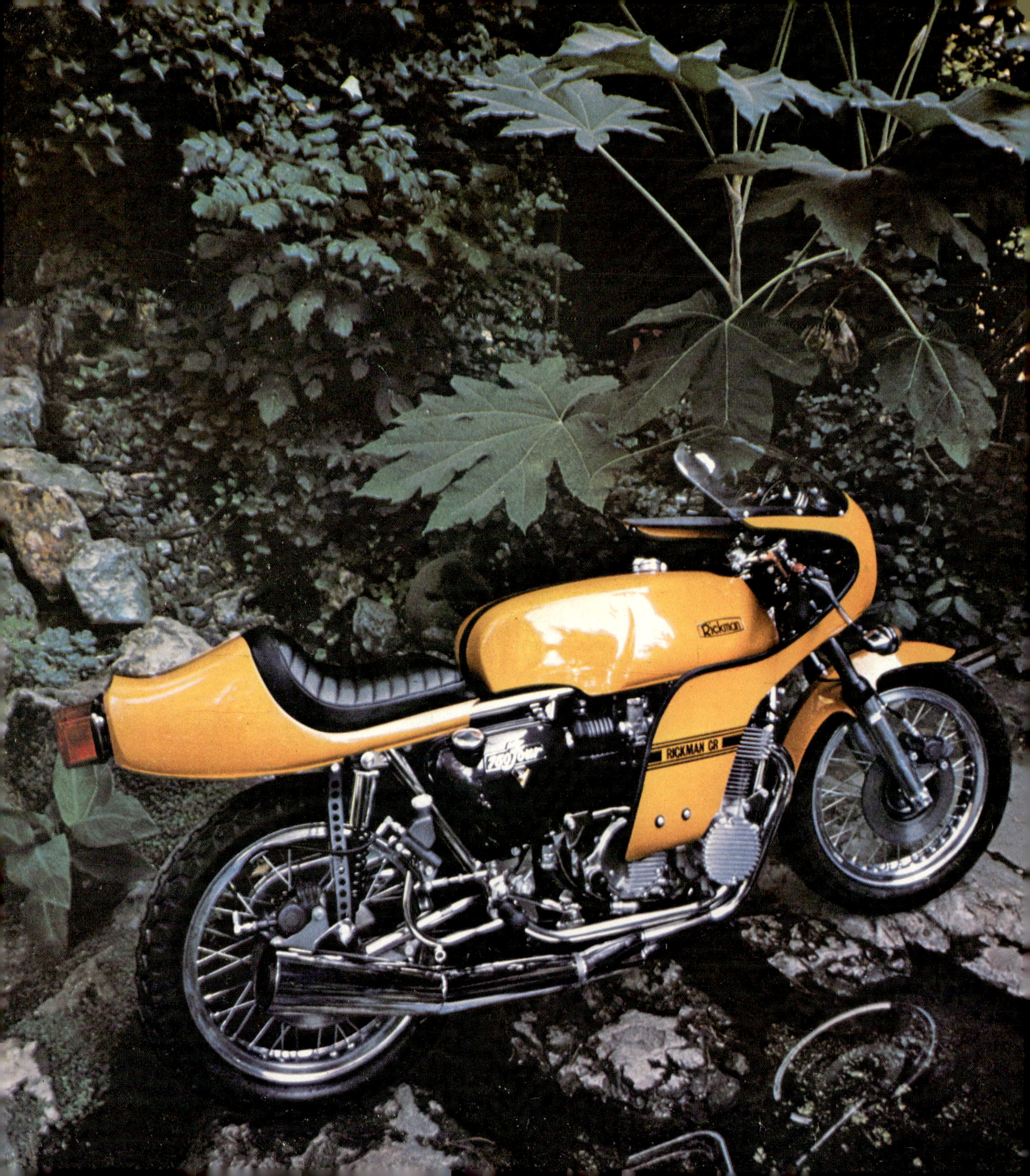
Rickman
RICKMAN CR

Rickman-Honda 750

Maybe the flashiest of all café racer kits is the Rickman chassis for the Honda 750 Four. Built like all Rickman frames out of nickel-plated Reynolds 531 tubing, it shares the same general geometry that gives them all superb handling. The Lockheed disc brakes at front and rear, the alloy rims, the Girling shocks, the Dunlop tires, the Rickman forks—all of this is by now a formula that equates with unshakable stability under all conditions. The tank is the traditional and efficient Rickman unit, but the curvaceous rear seat and angular fairing are unique to the Honda CR chassis and come only in eye-popping International Orange. Like all Rickman chassis, it needs the engine/gearbox package, instruments, centerstand and sundry bits from the stock Honda to be complete, but it's a relatively minor work of assembly.

This particular machine was built by Max Gordon's International Cycles in San Jose, and features a well warmed-over Yoshimura engine with Kerker exhaust, no kickstarter and a plethora of finned accessory sidecovers. In this trim, it's a motorcycle to rival any in how it looks and how it goes. Few rival the Rickman-Honda when it comes to a head-to-head pricetag comparison, too, for the price of the complete machine is truly staggering. But then again, you could never do it so well all by yourself.

Kawasaki H-2 750

Max Gordon's in San Jose is also the home of this highly unusual and strikingly pretty Kawasaki 750 Triple. A real road burner, the stock "Kwacker" is definitely *not* noted for its handling, although when it comes to acceleration and top speed, few bikes of any size can touch it. This bike retains the stock "rubber frame," but it does have reworked forks at the front and Koni shocks fitted with Tim Witham's springs at the rear. It's also a lot lighter, and the rider sits much further back. So handling—while not radically changed—is considerably improved.

So is the styling. A huge molded marshmallow of a tank hovers over the engine, exhibiting hefty cutouts at the rear to give the rider someplace for his knees. The traditional domed racing seat matches up perfectly for shape and function, as do the minimal rear fender and Manx Norton-style front gravel catcher. Custom headlight brackets, clip-ons and rear-sets complete this straightforward chassis and give it a fleet, exciting look. The engine is plenty exciting as it comes from the factory, and except for expansion chambers, not much has been done to it . . . or needs to be.

Dick LaPlante of San Gabriel has a 750 Kawasaki remarkably similar to Max Gordon's. Once again, both front and rear suspension have been refined, though this Triple is shod with aesthetically pleasing but mediocre Goodyear Eagle tires that are known more for their durability than handling. The tank, seat and front fender are all bits from Dick's Cycle West, as is the rather silly and awkward head fairing. And all are painted in that distinctive, soft-white, pearlescent color which is LaPlante's trademark. The rear-sets and clip-ons are his own products, while the chambers are from J&R. Velocity stacks without filters are the only other performance improvement, but the bike goes more than adequately, nonetheless.

Kawasaki H-2 750

Laverda 750 SFC

Aesthetically, the Italian Laverda SFC has it all over any other factory café racer. This is one beautiful motorcycle, from the subtle silvery backbone frame to the flamboyant International Orange racing fiberglass. And the quality is fantastic. The single overhead cam 750cc Laverda Twin is reminiscent of Honda's legendary 305 Super Hawk—though pumped up to double size. In the racing trim of the SFC, it's rated at 75 horsepower, good for nearly 140 mph. Originally designed to win the prestigious 24-hour Bol D'Or production road race, the SFC is incredibly sturdy, with excellent German

Bosch electrics (including electric starter), Tomaselli clip-ons, Ceriani forks, TT-100 tires and three disc brakes. Instruments are the same reliable gauges used on Honda Fours.

Selected from all over the world, this grab bag of high class components has been craftily blended together with infinite care and workmanship to produce the only real competitor for Ducati's Super Sport. It's not quite as fast, not quite as stable, not quite as technologically advanced as the big "Duck." But, on the other hand, it's much less expensive . . . not to mention a lot prettier.

MV Agusta Sport 750

Like Enzo Ferrari builds automobiles, Count Agusta of MV builds motorcycles. That is to say, the finest possible means of carrying a highly skilled rider from here to there in safety and as fast as it is possible to go. It may not be comfortable, but you'll never forget that trip . . . ever. Chances are, most riders will never even have the chance to ride an MV Agusta 750 Sport around the block, for there are only a few dozen in the country, and when they change hands, the price is apt to be whatever the owner feels like charging . . . and up. But whatever the cost, just the supernatural exhaust note is worth every precious penny.

Every component is a hand-built work of art in itself, and taken as a whole, the 750cc four-cylinder, four-carburetor, double overhead cam, 130 mph chassis is perhaps the most visceral way of traveling across the land that man has yet devised. Derived from many times world championship MV Grand Prix bikes, the 750 Sport is a barely civilized racer. Its only imperfection is the poorly applied garish paint job that disguises truly beautiful, traditional Italian lines. But that is the mere quibble of a connoisseur. If it was perfect, it would be only a machine. Mildly flawed, the MV Agusta is a true monument of modern art.

MV Agusta 750 America

If the MV Agusta Sport is the ultimate Italian motorcycle, then the MV Agusta 750 America is the ultimate Italian-American bike. Chris and Armando Garville—the new MV importers—have taken the demanding Sport and revamped it thoroughly for American conditions. The result is a bike that's prettier, more exotic and maybe even better. The styling is all new, with a squared-off, breadloaf tank and a wonderful suede seat with adjustable backrest. This little gizmo slides back and forth to make a perfectly located solo saddle or a comfortable dual seat at the flick of a wing nut.

The mechanicals of the America are mostly the same as the Sport, and pretty much identical to MV's racing 500s, for that matter. But the minor controls are better. And things like air cleaners, heavier fork tubes, double disc front brakes, excellent electrics and decent paint are all welcome improvements. The tank decals still wash off in the first rain, but that happens on any Italian machine. Whether it should when the price is nearly $7,000 is a matter open for discussion, but there's no argument that if any factory-built motorcycle is worth more than most cars, this should be the one.

photo courtesy of Doug Mesney

Norton Commando 750 Production Racer

Of all the motorcycles Norton has built in the last seventy years, one of the most beautiful models is surely the sublime Commando 750 Production Racer of 1969/1971. Built in very limited quantities, these yellow wonders were the first production Nortons with front disc brakes. The frame is the stock Norton Isolastic unit, which suspends the inherently shaky, old long-stroke Twin in rubber donuts for uncanny smoothness, while giving even better handling than the famous Featherbed frame upon which Norton built its modern reputation. The defrosted engine has full race cams, big Amal carbs and a huge oil cooler.

With special versions of Norton's own superb forks, Dunlop tires, alloy rims and a Metisse-style fiberglass fender, the front end is a paragon of classic British road-racing technology. An alloy rim, Koni shocks and a matching Dunlop upgrade the rear wheel to similar specs. Rear-sets mounted on lovely aluminum plates and clip-ons take care of the rider controls. The distinctive, streamlined fiberglass was developed in conjunction with Paul Dunstall, and is available in replica sets from Max Gordon's. It's better looking than Dunstall's own glass, with a fullness, roundness and integration of line that truly complements the traditionally good-looking Norton engine. Aside from its mechanical sophistication, the Commando 750 has to be one of the prettiest cycles yet devised.

Norton Commando 750 Production Racer

Phil Schilling, executive editor of *Cycle* magazine, is a great collector of classic racing machines. Sensing that the Norton Production Racer was going to be a real collector's item, in 1970 he had Peter Williams—Norton's wizard development engineer—personally build him the ultimate Commando. The price was outrageous, of course, but so is the result.

The engine is much wilder than that in the more mundane versions, with a veritable host of trick parts—not the least of which is a Quaife 5-speed gearbox. Full megaphone exhausts are fitted, along with gigantic Amal carbs. The fork sliders and internals have been reworked for superior damping and the fender has been trimmed. Otherwise, the front end is basically like that on all the Commando racers. At the rear, the swingarm bushing has been totally revised, and the arm itself lengthened.

Myriad other small improvements that only the factory development chief would know to do make this the highest possible refinement of the Commando chassis. More obvious is the deeply skirted tank, with a fuel capacity of a full 6.0 gallons. It's not as attractive as the standard Production Racer tank, but it does take full advantage of every performance possibility. And that of course, is what makes this the finest 750 Norton Commando ever built.

Seeley-Norton 750

Frank Reps of Los Angeles is a very opinionated cyclist. And this is his highly individualistic proposal for a lightweight, big-bore café racer. Built around an impossibly heavy and old-fashioned Norton Twin, the complete machine weighs less than 350 pounds—or about the same as a Yamaha 350, the lightest of the Japanese small-bore machines. To achieve this incredible weight, Reps used a truss frame built by Colin Seeley that cantilevers the big Norton engine out from the crucial swingarm pivot, with no downtubes to distribute the load. But handling is fantastic. Unlike the Commando, however, the Seeley frame demands that the Norton Twin be bolted tightly in place, with the inevitable result that the whole machine vibrates insanely. With little weight to pull, the engine has been left in a mild state of tune, with only Dunstall's patented Power Exhaust to give it a bit of boost.

The remainder of the chassis is basically British Traditional—Norton forks, Girling shocks, Dunlop tires, Lockheed disc brakes front and rear, alloy rims, Reynolds chain, Manx Norton front fender. The small gas tank and seat are sprint-racing bits made by Seeley, and the rear-sets are by Reps and use Heim joints on the control linkages. The wide, flaring clip-ons are also his own handiwork. Like everything else on the machine, they're top quality . . . and distinctly different.

This fantastic Triumph Trident is a bit more than a mere café racer. Now owned by Max Gordon of International Cycle Sales, it was built by the factory for the 1971 Daytona 200 and extensively campaigned by Gene Romero in AMA Nationals. To duplicate, it would take something over $25,000, though it's now obsolete for top caliber racing. Max has been known to crank it up and blast around the streets of San Jose, however, breaking eardrums for miles.

The full race 750cc Triple has every conceivable racing modification, and puts out close to 100 hp—enough for a 160 mph top speed with Daytona gearing. Dunlop tires are fitted on alloy rims, held on by Koni shocks and modified Triumph forks. Double front discs and a single rear platter on custom brackets—plus handmade rear-sets, exhaust system and all controls—add to the construction expense. The tank and seat are modified Rickman Metisse, while the fairing is one of the earliest with a horizontal air intake across the nose to feed internal ducting to provide additional downforce at high speeds.

A big, unwieldly racer in its heyday, it's an impressive mantelpiece racer now. Hardly street legal, it's still a blast just to start and feel the tremendous power envelop you in an impenetrable halo of sound and vibration.

Triumph Trident 750

Moto Guzzi 850 Sport

Moto Guzzi's 850 Sport is the latest mutation of their popular factory café racer introduced originally as a mount for Bol d'Or production racing. The transverse V-twin Guzzi—now bored out to 850cc in all models—is perhaps the sturdiest of all motorcycle engines, having started life as the motive force behind a proposed mini-truck for NATO forces in Europe. This 75 hp pushrod wonder —complete with 5-speed gearbox—is shoehorned into a lovely triangulated frame, fitted out with the best components you can buy, from double disc front brakes to alloy rims, from Bosch electric starter to reliable shaft drive. The unique clip-ons are adjustable for height and reach, the foot controls can be switched from side to side and the fuel taps even close electrically when the ignition key is withdrawn.

It may not be the fastest café racer in Italy, but the Guzzi will corner with the best of them, carry two people without hassles and delight the appreciative motorcycle aesthete with both the quality of its workmanship and the beauty of its design. Unlike many café racers that make substantial compromises in the name of style, the Guzzi Sport has more class than most people can handle.

The original British hot rodder, Paul Dunstall, has been successfully modifying big bore machines into production racers for over a decade. He is still most famous for his nickel-rocket Dunstall Domiracer. The current Dunstall Nortons are out of the same mold. Based on the standard Norton 850 Commando, Dunstall's version adds a few horsepower through high compression pistons, a hotter cam and his own patented two-into-one-into-two crossover exhaust system which ends in Dunstall patented silencers. The rear-sets, clip-ons and control levers are Dunstall, too, as is all the fiberglass work. Noted neither for its durability nor its looks, the true Dunstall fiberglass from England is usually replaced in this country by American-made replicas for longer life. As a complete machine or a kit, the Dunstall Norton (and similar Triumph and Honda café racers) is about the closest you can come to a real British "street scratcher" without building it up yourself.

Dunstall Norton 850

Norton John Player Special 850

The yellow Norton Production Racers of a few years ago are among the classics of our time. But it's hard to see the same respect being accorded to the John Player Special. Built out of a stock Commando 850, it's been widely acclaimed as a very high-class machine. The JPS Norton is easily the most refined of all machines to come out of Andover. But primarily it's a styling exercise, for the chassis is mostly unchanged. And unless there's an aesthetic revolution coming right around the corner, the unusual styling of the JPS will have limited appeal. The Avon fairing—one of the first with an inner liner to make it look as nice from the rider's point of view as from the pedestrian's—is heavily constructed. Indeed, English law now requires metal gas tanks, so the thick fiberglass you see is really only a cover for a standard Commando tank. Similar hefty construction is evident throughout, and the black chrome exhausts are extremely attractive. But that fat fairing with two eyes may take some getting used to.

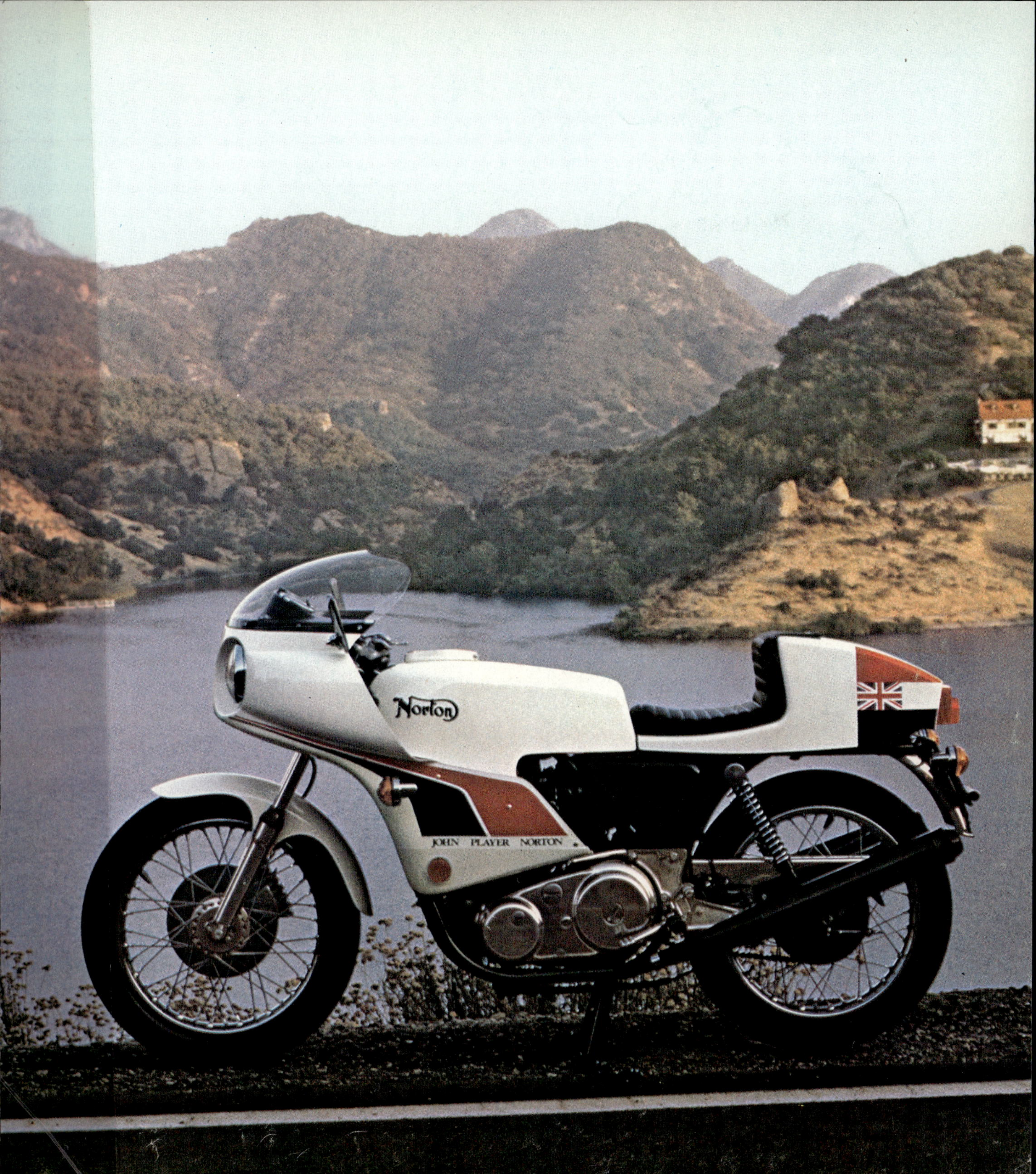
Norton
JOHN PLAYER NORTON

BMW R90S

The BMW R90S is an eccentric factory café racer. The lumbering old Flat-twin is far from graceful but will wind over 7000 rpm, run nearly 130 mph and do the quarter in the low 13s. The two-passenger seat is wonderfully comfortable, the head fairing is solid, effective and pretty, the fancy ventilated double discs work superbly and stock BMW features—like shaft drive, a full instrument panel that even includes a clock and magnificent workmanship throughout—make the R90S one of the best motorcycles you can buy. It's not a cobbled-up factory racer, but a well-considered exercise in the art of going fast on two wheels. Of course, it also costs over $4,000. But then, there's nothing else you have to add to make it what you want. It's complete, tested and thought out as it comes from the factory—a café racer ready to be ridden.

Not as fancy as many big café machines, this Kawasaki Z-1 of Max Gordon's has a nice little Rickman bikini fairing, Koni shocks, a set of Dunlop TT 100s, custom-built rear-sets that also mount passenger pegs, clip-ons, a protective set of Dyno-Gards in case of a spill and a Kerker four-into-one exhaust. That innocent-looking Z-1 engine, however, actually displaces over 1000cc and has been built up to full-race specs by none other than Pops Yoshimura. It originally went to Daytona as a Kawasaki record setter and returned covered with high-speed glory. Even when plugged into this mild-mannered, mostly stock Z-1, it has run 160 mph. And it will blast through the quarter-mile at about 130 mph in the low 11s. For a street playbike with a stock frame, that's going some.

Kawasaki Z-1 900

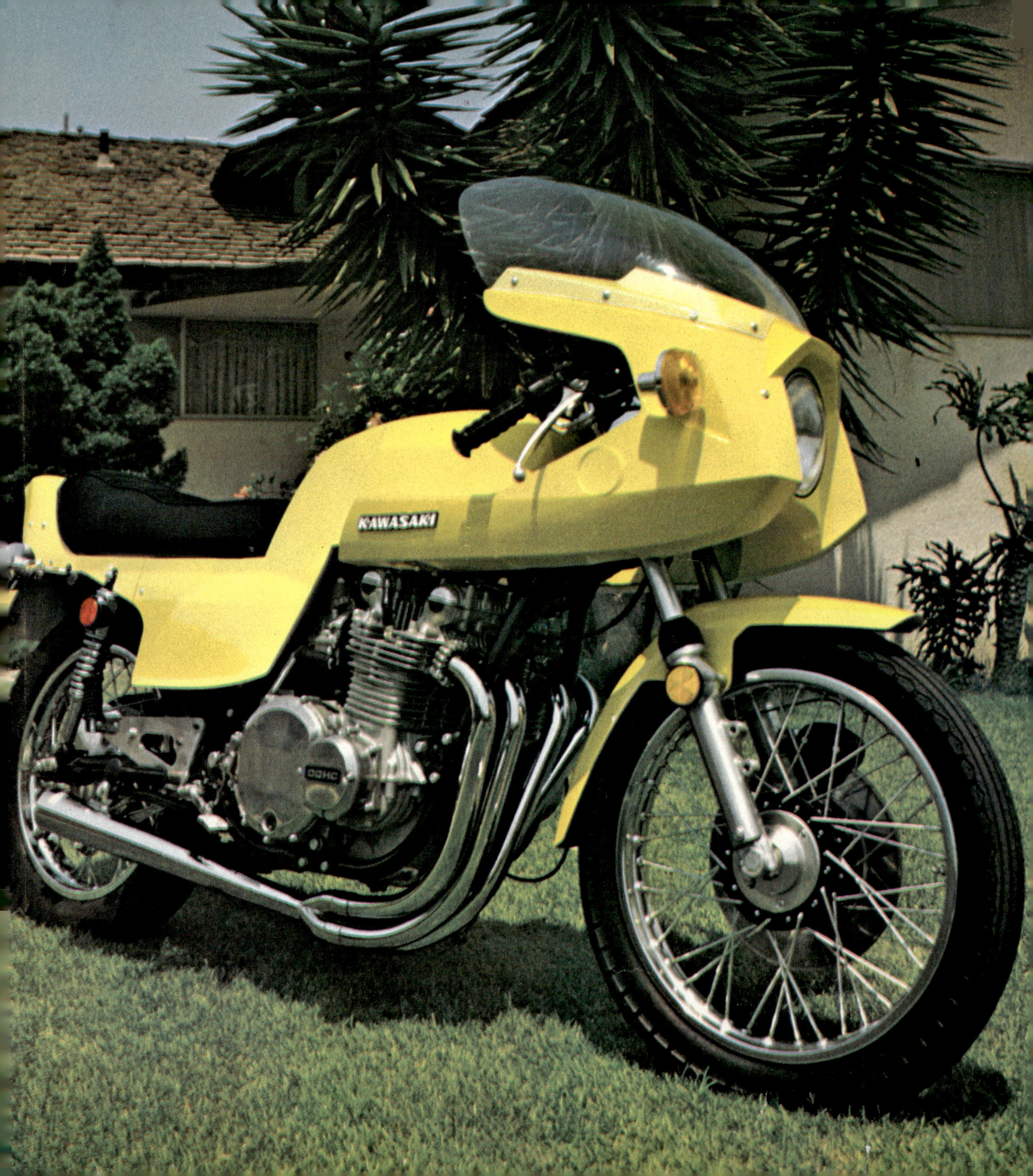
KAWASAKI
DOHC

Built by K&N Engineering in Riverside, this 900 Z-1 Kawasaki uses Dunstall's fancy factory fiberglass kit as the basis for a real attention getter that's more flash than substance. A Kerker four-into-one, custom rear-sets and clip-ons are the extent of chassis changes. But the entire proportion of the bike has been altered with the one-piece seat/tank combo, fairing and front fender. Like all Dunstall fiberglass, this curious mixture is aimed at creating straight lines where logic says there should be curves. Chisel edges, broken sweeps, a hexagonal surround for the headlight—everywhere you look there's another quirky styling feature. Even the front fender is as near as you can get to a square and still have it fit around a tire. The "total look" seat/tank means doors had to be left in order to reach the fuel taps, and the steering lock has been reduced to near zero. It's a very distinctive—though totally impractical—bike, well outside the mainstream of even **rarefied** café racer development.

Kawasaki Z-1 900

In every field there's an ultimate—the very best. The Rickman-Kawasaki is that café racer. The frame is a variant of the nickel-plated Metisse drawn up by Don and Derek Rickman over a decade ago. Stiff enough to be a race frame, it's triangulated like a bridge girder and engineered with all the perfection you'd expect from something that's the combined result of computerized stress analysis and British road testing.

With this rock-steady foundation to work from, it's only a matter of adding exactly the right bits and making them work in harmony to come up with the ultimate café racer. The front forks are Rickman-built Ceriani copies; the disc brake comes from Rickman, too. The alloy rim carries a fat TT 100, while the instruments and gauges are straight Z-1. At the rear, another chunky Dunlop on an alloy rim —complete with hydraulic rear disc—connects to that lovely frame with a set of carefully balanced Girlings. The exquisite rear-sets, clip-ons and bright green/yellow fiberglass bits are all from the Rickman factory, and like the frame, have a reputation for being the best.

The Z-1 engine is virtually legendary at this point, and a Yoshimura version even more so. The 984cc, full-race Yoshimura motor in this particular Rickman was put together by Jack O'Malley of Orient Express Motorcycles on Long Island, and the day after it was assembled ran 146 mph. The only part that's not either Kawasaki or Yoshimura is the Kerker exhaust, but like the rest of this machine, it's also the best in its field.

Rickman-Kawasaki Z-1 900

Laverda 1000 Triple

One of the most understated—but also perhaps the best—of all factory café racers is the exotic Laverda 1000. Everything about it is truly first class, from the excellent Italian double downtube frame to the double disc front brakes, the Borrani rims to the 80 hp double overhead cam 980cc Triple, the Tomaselli controls to Dunlop tires, the German Bosch electrics to Japanese instruments, the Ceriani forks to Ceriani shocks, the oversized headlight to equally oversized padded café racer dual seat. For the mature enthusiast, the demurely styled Laverda will run just a blink over 125 mph, do the quarter-mile in under 13 seconds at 106 mph and outhandle its production racer 750 SFC sibbling. It's about the same price as the flashy Ducati Super Sport 750, but performs with a solidity and refinement that the highly-stressed V-twin just can't match. It will carry two passengers comfortably—though still utilizing rear-sets—and can be relied on to go cross country in style and comfort. It may not be everyone's choice as the high-dollar ultimate café racer, but it has to be pretty close.

Café Racer Address List

Barney Tillman's Dunstall Sport Center
6027 Whittier Boulevard
Los Angeles, Calif. 90022

Bates Industries
700 West 16th Street
Long Beach, Calif. 90801

BMW
Butler & Smith
Walnut and Hudson
Norwood, N.J. 07648

Dick's Cycle West
304 Agostino Road
San Gabriel, Calif. 91776

Ducati
Berliner Motor Corp.
Plant Road and Railroad Street
Hasbrouck Heights, N.J. 07604

Fibercraft
3221 20th Street
San Francisco, Calif. 94100

American Honda
100 West Alondra
Gardena, Calif. 90247

International Cycle Sales
1615 Almaden Road
San Jose, Calif. 95125

Interpart Corp.
100 Oregon Street
El Segundo, Calif. 90245

Kawasaki Motors
1062 McGaw Avenue
Santa Ana, Calif. 92705

K & N Engineering
Box 1329
Riverside, Calif. 92502

Laverda
Continental Motorcycles
153 Ludlow Avenue
Northvale, N.J. 07647

Moto Guzzi
Premier Motor Corp.
Railroad Street and Plant Road
Hasbrouck Heights, N.J. 07604

MV Augusta
The Garville Corp.
200 Clearbrook Road
Elmsford, N.Y. 10523

Norton
Berliner Motor Corp.
Plant Road and Railroad Street
Hasbrouck Heights, N.J. 07604

Orient Express Motorcycles, Inc.
399 West Sunrise Highway
Freeport, N.Y. 11520

Racecrafters International
7932 Sunset Strip
Hollywood, Calif. 90046

Rickman
Triumph-Norton
2745 East Huntington
Duarte, Calif. 91010

Rube Goldberg Distributing
3686 South Main
Los Angeles, Calif. 90007

Triumph-Norton
2745 East Huntington
Duarte, Calif. 91010

Yamaha International
6600 Orangethorpe
Buena Park, Calif. 90620

WATERLOO LOCAL SCHOOL
MIDDLE SCHOOL LIBRARY

CAFE RACERS
629 TAY.   37497

TAYLOR,RICH

37497